BIRDS

TO PAINT
OR COLOR

Dot Barlowe

DOVER PUBLICATIONS, INC.
Mineola, New York

Note

What richness comes to us from the birds around us! How much poorer our world would seem without their colors and their songs! In every picture in this book, the skilled wildlife artist Dot Barlowe shows her love for these creatures—a love you will share as you add color to her pictures. (See the inside back cover for a Color Guide.) This book is unlike a standard coloring book, because it allows you to remove and save each page you have colored. (Be sure to follow the perforated lines.) Because Dot Barlowe's drawings are printed very lightly, the lines will hardly be noticeable when you have finished painting or coloring. When your picture is finished, you can put it in a frame and hang it on your wall or give it to someone you love. It will be a unique, original work of art that will give you pleasure every time you look at it!

Copyright

Copyright © 2007 by Dover Publications, Inc.
All rights reserved.

Bibliographical Note

Birds to Paint or Color is a new work, first published by Dover Publications, Inc., in 2007.

DOVER *Pictorial Archive* SERIES

This book belongs to the Dover Pictorial Archive Series. You may use the designs and illustrations for graphics and crafts applications, free and without special permission, provided that you include no more than four in the same publication or project. (For permission for additional use, please write to Permissions Department, Dover Publications, Inc., 31 East 2nd Street, Mineola, N.Y. 11501.)

However, republication or reproduction of any illustration by any other graphic service, whether it be in a book or in any other design resource, is strictly prohibited.

International Standard Book Number: 0-486-45171-2

Manufactured in the United States of America
Dover Publications, Inc., 31 East 2nd Street, Mineola, N.Y. 11501

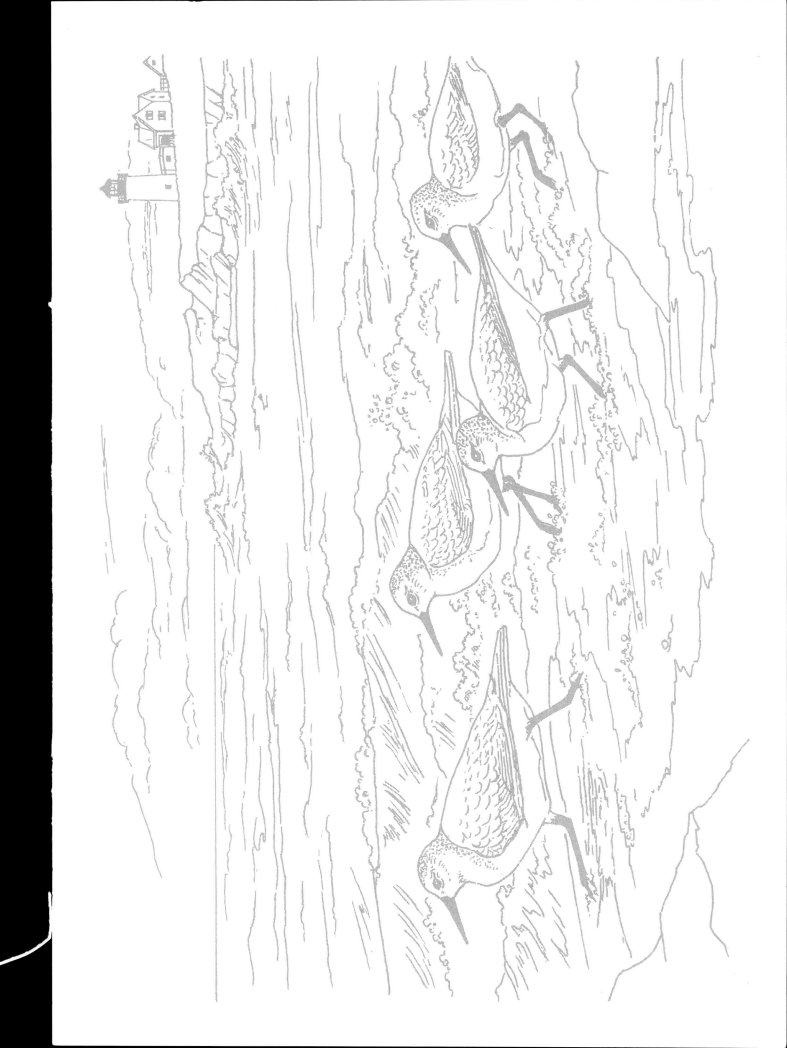